This journal belongs to:

Star Power Publishing

Hattiesburg, Mississippi

YOU
ARE
AMAZING

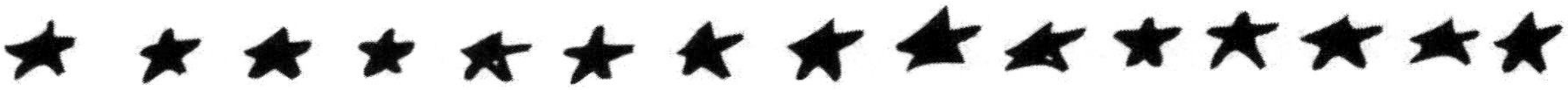

★ ★ ★ ★ ★ ★ ★ ★ ★ ★ ★ ★ ★ ★ ★

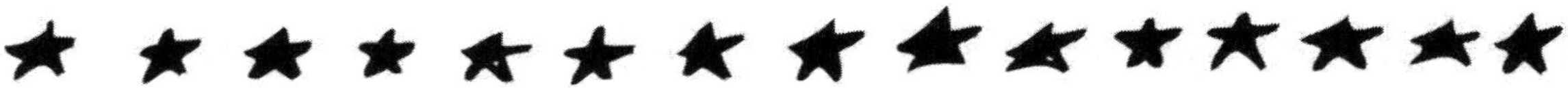

★ ★ ★ ★ ★ ★ ★ ★ ★ ★ ★ ★ ★ ★ ★

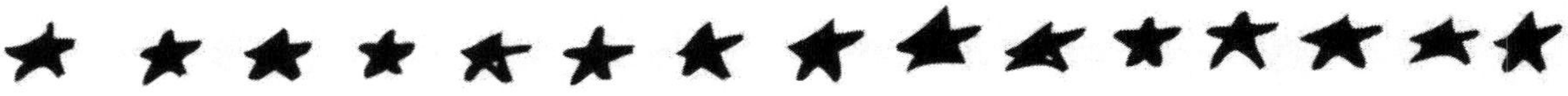

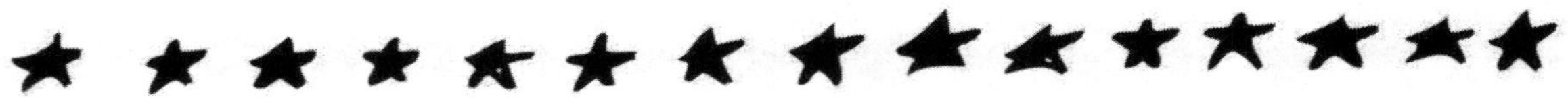

★ ★ ★ ★ ★ ★ ★ ★ ★ ★ ★ ★ ★ ★ ★

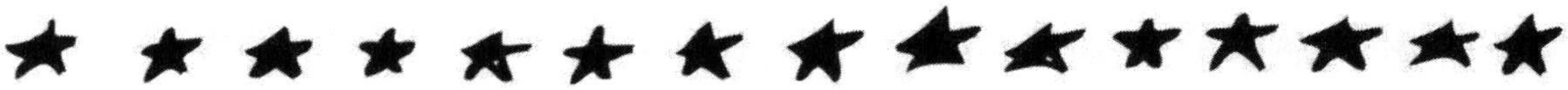

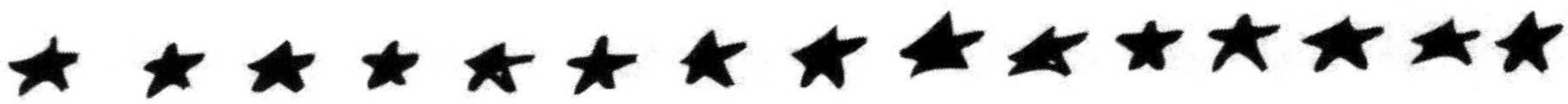

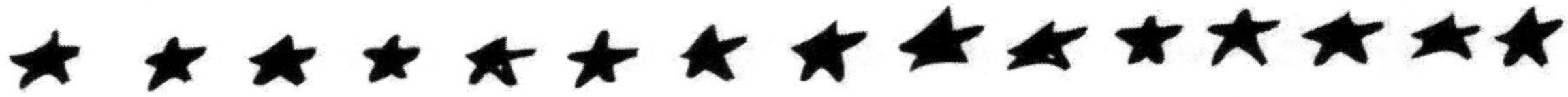

Printed in Great Britain
by Amazon

17316654R00061